There will be
days
that matter.

Today.

The birthday
of your mother.

All the days
between.

Wiener Dogs and Other Muses

poems

by Christine Hoper

Whitney!
Every day...
your day
:) Christine

Special Thanks

Denise Knudson
Julie Walnum & Pura Larson
Rochelle & Emily Durgin
John Powers
Renee LaMie
Kris Kerzman
Kevin Carollo
Spider Johnk
Janelle Berge
Punchgut
Betsy Stadick
Kevin Tobosa
Eden Parker

& all the Muses

Traffic
To the Grumpy Man in the
  Underground Parking Lot
Gravy
Toaster Oven
Brussels Sprouts
What I Love Best About Sundays
Ode to Bacon
…the Heroine
…the Reader
…the Photograph
…the Truth
…Technology
Possible Obsessions
Club Soda

February, i
March
Today, iii
Midnight, that May
July
Time Flies
Summer, ii
Morning Coffee
August
Like Today
September 17
Haiku
Jade
Santa
Stay, i
February, ii

Crab
iPoem
Daily I Fall in Love with Words
Mailbox
Now, ii
Fun and Games
Gifts
Remember
Farm Truck
Recipe for Keys
To The Guy at the Poetry
  Reading Who Ran Into My Eye
Trains on Loon Lake
For Jair
You, iv
Loaded

Stay, iii
Like Dragonflies
Calico
Return, i
Return, ii
Coming Up
Somewhere, i
Find
Before Me
Broken Dreams
Now, i
For Kate

I could eat you

but I'd still be so hungry

for you...

give peace a chance
moon. and poppies too.
and stardust.
and guava.
and tic-tac-toe.

Traffic

I saw you
walking home late
afternoon. Maybe
after dinner
at your mother's.

Looking right.
Then left. Before
crossing to close the last
block.

I wonder, if she served
mashed potatoes.
Your mother.

If she knew
the wind
was not the first, today
to sift your curls.

Kiss
your cheek.

To the Grumpy Man in the Underground Parking Lot

Don't worry. We will squeeze the
bitter out of you and use it
to make Grandma's German chocolate
cake.

Your not-to-be-bothered glare will taste
simply delicious
with milk.

Your *humpf* to our greeting is
dark chocolate chips–the extra twice
chocolate-in-chocolate.

Your frown will be frosting, grown firm
at the edges.
Waiting to be bitten.

In the days before we learn
what you have learned,
you will be our favorite after-school treat.

Even the dog will beg
to lick the plate.

Gravy

Might be difficult
on some accounts, not Nana's.
All you do is add a little pepper dear...
she'd say *and pass the peas,* and
fill your plates...

This year Nana's chair
sits empty. Save the weight
between the passing of meat and glazed
carrots and raisin cream pie and
the planting and digging and
bearing of children and
planting and freezing and thawing
and digging and living and dying and
thanking and planting and digging
and losing and finding and laughing and
holding back tears and still trying and
planting and thanking and digging
and eating and passing the meat and
potatoes.

The sum
of what a lifetime
can be.

Here.
In the space you have today.
The rest is
gravy.

Toaster Oven

Ready for heat
at a moment's notice. You tick
as you're warming, tempting
our noses.

You know we can't wait long to
taste of. And chew.
So you burn up our tongues
like you always do.

Stainless steel.
On the counter. So full
of hot lovin'.

Darned if you can't be all
or nothin'.

Toaster oven.

Brussels Sprouts

A roll
in a roll
of a tuck
in a fold
of a bonsai
cabbage leaf.

What I Love Best About Sundays

Is the perfectly, perfectly
perfectly round,
round, smooth skin, tight
sweet cool
I can roll

on my tongue just to roll,
roll, bite, chew into
pieces of heaven.

Is when you say
One end, stem,
five-tip star
at the other–
Not round.

Is when I say
That may be.

But what
I love best
about Sundays...

are the blueberry, blueberry,
blueberry
kisses

from you.

Ode to Bacon

And how we all know you'll take one
(or in truth twenty-five)
when the pan passes by
with such crispy deliciousness catching
your eye...

Whether candied in maple
or just set on the table
there's no better treat—
peppered, sizzling, fried, baked, wrapped, stuffed,
shoved inside
of your mouth when it's
hot and it's fresh and we
secretly wish we had
boxes and crates and
a hundred-some plates
for an ongoing feast of this
salty, cured meat
that we

can
not
stop
cravin'.

Bacon.

...the Heroine

Every book needs a heroine. The chapters of
history would yellow and crack without them.
Western border towns would shiver in their
river bottoms and not know why. Eastern
skies would empty their pockets of blue.

Librarians believe in heroines. They know why
heroines catching your stare, stare right back
and invite you in. Dreams are more memorable
with heroines. As are laundry rooms, bimini tops
and just around the corner.

Heroines have vices. Seductive charms.
Whiskey. Many of them wear shirts with
snaps and familiar patterns. They are not
afraid to cry uncontrollably in the middle of
dinner. With or without wasabi.

...the Reader

The reader knows everything about the
Heroine. When not reading or within earshot
of other readers, the reader refers to
the heroine's favorite songs, foods and
movies as if they were the reader's own. As if
the heroine stepped out of line to dodge a
bullet and the reader closed the gap.

The reader comes from a long line of listeners
who took up reading when words became
flesh. For that reason, there are days the
reader goes without reading. Or sleep.

Sometimes, the reader imagines the heroine
staring back across the fire.

...the Photograph

The photograph will grow on you. Slowly at
first, then blossom in the dead of Winter like a
Jade. One day, you'll realize the photograph
has been studying you. Watching you come
and go. Knitting as you wash dishes.
Rearranging blankets on the couch. Idling.
Yesterday, it followed you outside. To the
edge of the fire.

The photograph is never distracted by
heroines, however old-fashioned, ill-fated or
shrewd. It is content to watch you read.

It would be nice if the photo would stop.
Maybe a restraining order. But to what end?
The photograph swallowed you long ago, along
with a thousand words.

...the Truth

The truth can be hard to put a finger on. Like
a trigger. Only not a trigger. Because everyone
knows the reader will get the last word.

Not the girl.

...Technology

Being framed in a book is not the end of
things. Even when the cover closes. And the
lights go out. Paragraphs mingle and whisper
in tongues. Send text messages.

The heroine knows.

Possible Obsessions

Families of pens with none known missing.
Anything reversible.
Candy corn.
Not-too-slippery-not-too-sticky lip gloss.
Stickers.
Alphabets.
Turquoise domino sets.
Russian nesting dolls.
Buttons from my mother.
Skeleton keys.
Midnight.
Night lights.
Mini cat's-eye marbles.
Brushed metal.
Families of pens with none known missing.

Club Soda

It's the way that your bubbles
effervesce the days troubles
and convert perfect strangers to kin.

How you giggle and dance
on your way down the hatch

to mingle with
tangerine friends.

How you marvel the luck–
being un-bottled up

with nothing but
white space
to hold 'ya.

Club soda.

A day will come

to walk North...

some days…

I'd like
to pack the things that
matter most
in one
small bag and find
a bike
and ride.

February

i.

When I was young
I wore my hair in braids
and sang

and maybe I thought
about you
in my song
and maybe I cut up the sky
in my song
and maybe I did
and maybe it's gone

and when I was young
I wore my hair in braids
and sang

Now I am old
and my son wants to know
your name

March

I will rise
to meet you
said the river
courtesy
at your door

I follow as you
follow
said the moon

to tell or
not
to tell
said time all but
forgotten

I will pull you
even closer
said the moon

I will open a bank
said the river
take you
swimming, keep
a rope swing
in the safe

a thousand
minute hands
bells, tolls, ticks, clocks,
alarms said time
come rest here
in my arms

I am only
passing by
said time

I see you
said the moon
I see you look
again

sink
into life
said the river

ghosts of trees
and goddesses
are knocking
said the river let
them in

close your eyes
said the moon
rewind, rewind,
rewind

count me
I am yours
said time
spend me
you are
mine

hold all that floats
in common
said the river
undo
becomes undone

let me
take your turn
said the moon

in time
you will find
said time

Today
iii.

To you,
they are black t-shirts.
Who could ever need so many?

To me they are
late on Monday and
first-time client and
ignore this bad hair day and
celebrate because day and
casual day and
not my birthday and
the bosses birthday and
bring-your-daughter to work day and
not every day and
no daycare today and
last weekend and
lost weekends and
just back from Mardi Gras and
family vacation and
in need of time off day and
and the middle of Wednesday and
work in a workout and
in-between seasons and should maybe have
just called in sick day and
hooray for the team day and
it's raining again day and
we can pretend but it's still
not quite payday and if

time, being time,
forget this kiss,

then yes.

On that day, they will seem
like a stack of black t-shirts,
plus one.

Who could ever need so many?

Midnight, that May

My friend is beautiful
remembering
the house her
father built with room enough
for everyone, the walls
however
thin.

Even the wine
breathes easy.
Velvet
in our glasses as
she laughs,

invites us in.

She is
so beautiful,

my friend.

July

I watch for cowgirls
said the sky.

Kiss them all
before
they ride.

Time Flies

Growing suspicious
that the frequent flier miles
might be affecting her roots

platinum

Summer
ii.

No words for
Summer heat, no reason
to believe we
will not
find
reincarnation—

Let fingers
trace the way. Let
fingers weigh

The trace
of everything
left
to hold

come Winter.

Morning Coffee

The neighbor's
flower pots
stayed out all night.

Again.

Look at them.
Throwing up
their colors.

Even the shy
and quiet ones
have overdosed

on Summer.

August

Whispering Aspen.
Front porch creak.

Summer sounds I keep—

And keep.

Like Today

I remember walking to your dorm.
Knocking. How even your eyes
opened with the door.
How I told you he was
flying. Crashed.

Your sobs washed away
foundations. I didn't know
what to say.
Partly because I didn't know you.
Partly because I didn't know.

Because your parents
called my parents.
And I was a baton
passing you the brand-new empty.

We lost touch after
college. Except
for days

like today.

September 17

Today,
the wind is sleeping.

I am careful
not to wake her

but she stirs
and
mumbles as I pass.

Her breath smells like wine.

i.

thirty five pumpkins
in a plastic container
bite one. make a wish

ii.

everything on fire
wild geese
chasing where you kiss

iii.

another surprise
twins this time
babies five and six

Jade

Why do you insist on
turning inward? Branches
curving in the wrong
directions. Limbs
growing heavy until you are hard
to move.

At night we share
an armchair rest. Swaying with
the trains.

The newest leaves
are heart-shaped, green like Spring
and shiny.

Why do you insist
on turning
inward?

Santa

Ran into you last
Winter in
the stairwell. Full

of mistletoe and hurry, squeezing by
without recalling August
rain.

As if we wouldn't notice
Christmas.

Possessive of its season, of
exactly two flights
between
here,

and the rest of our lives.

Stay
i.

You are a late
snowfall.
Blanket of sleep
that won't
cover.

Sad because
no one
wants you
to stay.

Even the tolerant
shake their heads.
Sip coffee.
Say:

The sun will come and
float your mattress
out to sea.

February
ii.

I can find you
in a candle
in the jack and peel
of apple.

I can find you
in the fading light
of Fall.

I can find you
by the river
throwing skip-jacks back.

And you may not be
my first Love,

No.

But I can find you.

always sticky

stepping into you...

sometimes people ask about Jim
moon. and I really don't know what to say.
he's got a sweet spacesuit, likes
rødgrød med fløde—and I made him up one day.

(you know I knew better)
(but he's fun in this weather)

to infinity...

(and the john)

Crab

I love you crab.
with your scurry scurry tracks
of ghostwriting
in sand.

with your flurry of tasks
that of course you'll
get done.

with your hurry hurry claws
dig-dig-digging.

with your hurry hurry legs
side-step-stepping.

with your beady beady eyes
laser-sighting me, oh so
enticingly, watch-watch-watching me

watch you
right back.

I love you,
crab.

iPoem

I am looking for the girl who
turned
a block too early.

Who calls the 7:45 alarm
This time, forget it. Just get up.

Who loves
the smell of rain
before it rains.

I am looking
for the girl who leaves things

in your pockets.

Daily I Fall in Love with Words

*in response to Daily I Fall in Love with Mechanics by Susan Thurston, in
response to Daily I Fall in Love with Waitresses by Elliot Fried*

Daily I fall in love with words
with their heteronyms, antonyms, silent letters
WIND BOW STAND KNOW
and sources of origin.
I love how they fill up my ears
and slide into my eyes
jumping at me from pages
and street signs.
I feel their meaning
roughened by accents softened with whispers
slide over me.
Their double entendres
suggesting so…
fumbling and stuttering so sweetly
that I am left speechless, waiting.
Daily I fall in love with words
with their native languages.
They tell secrets in the paper
and I want them.
I know them.
They slip into history menus sermons songs–
their length long and short.
They have lovers or writers or tweeters
or all.

They are anciently worldly–
they know how civilizations speak.
Their careful arrangements form paragraphs
and clauses.
Daily I fall in love with words.
They are conveyors of dreams.
But they never remain in vacuum
as they sustain explain rearrange.

Mailbox

I miss you,
old mailbox. I miss your flag
in rusty red.

Your bent metal, thumb-wrestle
handle.

You brought us Sea
Monkeys. Seeds for
next Spring. Stamps
from strange countries
and lick-to-make-sticky
stamp hinges.

You were never
too full.

I miss you.

Paul always asks
if I need a ride home
and last night in the car
he told me how
his father's brother's
camper ran out of gas
at the top of a hill
and then coasted
just steps from
the station.

Now
ii.

I'd like to ask Paul
    to come in for a drink
    but I never ever do.
    Because I've had lots
    of thought
    on Paul,
    and I'm afraid I would
    probably

        say some.

Fun and Games

Suddenly,
there were
no more
fun
and

games.

Gifts

Words I found in a box
Out the back door
Beside a notebook
Next to the tracks
Believing they could fly.

Words I kept under my pillow.

Words I kicked out
Erased
Let go
Left by the side of the road.

Words I buried
Watered
Transplanted in an
Unsuspecting dream.

Remember

Remember when we never
combed our hair? Or thought
to eat?

When darkness smelled like
water lilies mixed with everything
but light?

Nothing could
wait.

You were every bit
an astronaut.

I was

just past sky.

Farm Truck

You are old,
farm truck. Traffic has
no time for you. Hay
bales, farmhands,
cattle,

gone.

I want to chase the suns
you've seen. Explore
your wooden panels—

Everything
that touched you.

I want to know
why sitting at
this stoplight
makes me
cry.

Recipe for Keys

My father had keys
and he gave some
to me.

Much better than
marbles
were skeletons,
masters, rusty, broken,
mysterious,
big, small, fat, bent,
tall keys—

Nancy Drew
secret-coded by
color and
notches and
foundry and
size.

Sift fingers through
them. Close
eyes, try to
find
what they open: safes,
padlocks, drawers, lockets,
old boxes and doors. Mix
them up
on a key ring.
Slide them off. Slide them
on. Keep them
with you.

When
grown-ups talk
grown-up, stare back
for as long
as you can while hands
deep inside pockets
make
key noises.

To The Guy at the Poetry Reading Who Ran Into
My Eye

First of all, I didn't know exactly how to address you, so let's just
say Ben.
And second,
I didn't mean to stare in the first place, but
there you were,
in the way of my eye.
Listening to
the poet,
which I was supposed to be listening to, too
but got caught up
in watching you.
I wanted to see
how the words got from the poems
into you. So I could sneak in behind
and
explore two or maybe three
parts of you, like
nowhere near
that tattoo,
and the hand holding
your notebook, and the space
someone else might have missed
below your knee—

But just one knee, Ben.
Because there is freedom in
not knowing.

Trains On Loon Lake

Train
whistles
after
midnight.

Moon
plays hide-and-seek
from lake to lake like
steel-gray rocks stuffed
in your nephew's pocket.

Slivers of darkness escape
to skip across the water.

Ripples only
if you see them. Echoes only
if you hear.

for Jair

There's something about
walking barefoot.

A feeling you just
can't beat.

I think it's the feeling
you get when you're feeling
the absence of
shoes

on your feet.

You
iv.

What I like about you is
your Not-a-Chance
laugh.

And the way
you say

…ten more
minutes.

Loaded

If you were
    an astronaut
    would you wink at me
    from space?

If you were
    a soda pop
    would you bubble
    in my face?

If you were
    a shortstop
    would you ever catch
    my eye?

And if
    I was a question would
    you ever
    ask me

    why?

cover heart's ears

cover heart's ears

cover heart's ears

where does special go to
moon? when does *I care* come out
not about you?

and who'd give the queen of hearts
a spade—then ask
(pretty please)

if she'll dig her own grave?

Stay
iii.

You are
an unexpected storm

a long ride home, slim chance
worth taking.

Even gracious hosts
won't ask you stay.

The Faithful
drive straight through.

Leave their clothes.

Rapture.

Like Dragonflies

Swarming into the future—
They could be pretty or
ugly as hell.

A silver battalion
charging the windows,
they try to get in
where the old ladies
separate string and the
old men sand wood blocks.

Mosquito hawks.
says one old woman.
We used them for bait
when I still had my leg.

Calico

The beginning is
never enough. Kisses
uncurl like
treasure maps keep

Secrets secret,
stowaways
along the path and

Anchors, always
anchors.

Reeling away
at your
calico heart.

Return
i.

Darkest dawn of
even
darker night.
Spanning wings
of angels caught
mid-flight.

Sprinkle dust
of bones from those
who leap–

Prayer blankets
now, for
secrets
held too deep.

Spellbound by trees
we walk
on riverbed
below.

No separation left, no
effort keeping
earthy mold
from promised
light.

Only faces.
Warmed by
memory
of you,

the
kindling

of life.

Return
ii

The gift I meant to send
to you
I opened.

Because you
are never coming back.

Even now
you are slipping through
the shadows like

a thousand
hexagons, I watch you
turn, divide and turn,
divide and
turn.

Remember
the harvest honeycombs?

...the end-of-Summer sweet
against our teeth?

You are never
coming back.

The gift I meant to send
to you

I opened.

Coming Up

This is
   a river.

   and this is how it
   smells.
   and this is how the rich, black soil piggybacks
   the water coming in and makes
   itself at home inside your home and
   laughs and swells and
   floats and coats last month's electric bill, the babysitter list, and
   all that good meat (plus a few things you hid) in the freezer.

   and these are
   the soggy pictures of your family with bits of
   dog food or maybe sand
   mixed in as you grab what you can
   swish-swash swishing.

   and this is you wading back in against
   the current and looking but not looking through the doorway
   wondering who and where and how to begin and
   this is your husband talking of
   desert climates and plant life and not liking clutter and
   you and your muddy-self wonder
        since when... and

Then.

You hear the Spring and the
water still moving, you notice the birds
have been chirping and all of you and
nature together are turning to the
sun and in the middle of the

water, water, water, *please, God,*
No
More
Water,
you are reminded of your
father and you realize there
will be mysteries for years and
years that seep into forever

and this –

This is

a river.

Somewhere
i.

Fall, sacred rain.
On cigarettes
and rainbow-colored cooler
cups.

Pool, sacred blood.
In bio-hazard altar
perched on Auntie's
counter.

Blow, sacred wind.
Carry ashes
of another limb
to Brother sky.

Roll, sacred river.
Wash our faces
when we cannot
cry.

Find

You may find yourself
throwing things away.

Underwear.
old photographs.
and
letters.

And just because a
stranger in an
airport says
he loves you,

You stay awake
at night.

And still find yourself
throwing things away.

Except
last year's tax return.
and
postcards.

Before Me

Before the
freeze and the
warming and the sailing and
exploring and marching
and the camps and the
conquering and
the burning and the
fighting and the claiming and
the rounding up and the
taking and wasting
and misplacing and the
assassination, indoctrination,
annihilation and
the bombing and the
theories and the stripping and
pumping and spilling and
polluting and the dust and the
floods and the fires
and the earthquakes and waves
and the leaks and reforms
and repeals and
the ratings and the
commentary and the slogans and
the text messages and the
panels and the
shouting and aligning and
misguiding and the
keeping apart and not telling
and the left out and
the far right and the sickness
in our middles and the
turning away and the
pointing and the land mines
and the others and the
not me and
the falling out of the sky and the
shooting,

We used to
take care of each other.

Broken Dreams

Like snowflakes slipping through the trees
on days in Fall it's not
supposed to snow.

Wandering as aimlessly
as ashes leave
a dying fire.

Not saying
what they've seen, they beckon
Sweetheart—
Love

and *See you there*

In the space where snowflakes
and ashes meet.

Broken dreams.

Now
i.

When you were
a doll, I
carried you.

When you were
a leaf I watched you green.
and gold.
and fall.

When you were my
lips, you were
in everything
I kissed.

Now you are
the quiet
after storm.

for Kate

Take careful stock of
empty. The room there is
to swim
in double spaces. Take

four strokes, breathe, take four
strokes, breathe,
take four strokes,
tuck, turn, breathe. Set

everything you've shouldered

out
to sea.

Christine Hoper is one of the most regular, quirky people you'll meet.

By day, she's been everything from a corporate trainer and marketing professional, to camp counselor and sunflower seed packing plant assembly line worker.

By night, she is a plant-lady, shoe collector, patron of the arts, cross country skier, and always a poet. The scribbling of thoughts in notebooks and on napkins goes back farther than she can recall.

A love of language and the spoken and written word defines her. Take her on in Scrabble, if you dare.

Christine is a native of the Midwest, having lived in a half-dozen small towns across the Red River Valley, Northwestern Minnesota, and Western North Dakota.

Today she makes her home in Fargo, ND. *Wiener Dogs and Other Muses* is her first published collection.

www.redrivergirl.com

Listening to

the full, full, full, so full of you
the drowning out of words of you
the heavy-to-the-top of you, the steel-on-
steel-on-wheels of you, the rusty clang, clang,
clank of you, the shaking air
and ground of you, the heat till red-hot
sound of you, the cars and crates
and squeaks and weight and chains and pops
and bangs and bright white
end-of-movie

space

that follows

in your place.